IF THE HOUSE IS INCLINED TO COLLAPSE

Casey Lynn Roland's poems manage to be intimate and revealing without having to give away what should not be given away. Something that was hidden in plain sight is suddenly made visible—nonetheless, a mystery continues to circulate below the surface. The inflections here sound plaintive, amused, querulous, accepting, insistent, but none of these tones is final or definitive. Roland's poems stick with you—they find a place in your soul, and in that way they are quite purposefully portable. You will carry them with you, dear reader. Lucky you! They travel well, and they are built for the long haul.

–DAVID RIVARD,
Some of You Will Know

In her debut collection, *If the House is Inclined to Collapse*, Casey Lynn Roland takes us on a tour of Massachusetts's North Shore, a landscape scarred by addiction. This is Roland's "coil-chained city," where a hard-earned sobriety is reflected in the light cast over this cold and rocky coastline, where "The Atlantic believes only in beginnings." I know this landscape all too well, and as I read this achingly beautiful account, found myself looking up and away, remembering, walking that first day of recovery, which is "every day. / A space filled with nothing . . . still a space / and still full." *If the House is Inclined to Collapse* transcends its pages as "the blue tinge of night drips onto us," and the dawn "could last forever."

–JENNIFER MARTELLI,
Psychic Party Under the Bottle Tree

Casey Roland is a poet with a vision of what it is to be a person who lives by poetry and works without myth in a mythologized landscape like her coastal towns north of Boston, the North Shore. She finds strength and loneliness in the hard-won ability to see the conditional fragmentary control and tragic possibility of the clause as well as the terns and gulls and sunlight. Her poems are kindred landscapes, sharp, real, twisty, metaphorical as well as real, and surprising.

–DAVID BLAIR,
Barbarian Seasons

It is a rare thing to deeply know a place and to be able to articulate it. Casey Lynn Roland knows the North Shore of Massachusetts, its houses and beaches, the way it feels to drive through the downtown at 2 a.m., the lure of the highway and the surf. She writes unironically about family ties and traditions, and with haunting reserve about addiction. These spare, atmospheric poems acknowledge how much our surroundings define us, how they reflect our loves and struggles. *If the House is Inclined to Collapse* is both profoundly personal and an important contribution to the literature of the North Shore.

–J.D. SCRIMGEOUR,
Poet Laureate of Salem, Massachusetts

IF THE HOUSE IS INCLINED TO COLLAPSE

Casey Lynn Roland

Fernwood
PRESS

If the House Is Inclined to Collapse

Fernwood Press
Newberg, Oregon
www.fernwoodpress.com

Printed in the United States of America

Cover and page design: Mareesa Fawver Moss
Cover photograph: Casey Lynn Roland
Author photo: Becky Jo Roland
Section header images: Ro Gavin

ISBN 978-1-59498-222-4

To Becky Jo, Mom, and Dad
and to the North Shore of Massachusetts

Contents

Many thanks to the editorial staffs of the following publications, where many of these poems first appeared, some in earlier forms:

The Bookends Review: "If the House Is Inclined to Collapse"
Harpur Palate: "Dementia Poem"
Plainsongs: "Barnacle"
Poets Choice: "Gold," "The Street Where We Lived Was Shaped Like a Horseshoe"
Red Ogre Press: "Highly Volatile Flammable Liquid"
Rougarou Journal: "In the Morning I am Sober and Can See"
Soundings East: "Sewing"
West Trade Review: "Watercolor"

Watercolor

Later, we watch everyone else get high
on the porch—tang of lime
still on our lips.
The moon making dim spotlights
through backyard leaves

turns grass to ocean floor
and obscures us in small shadows.

You smoke and nurse a beer, and
our knees finger-lock.
I forget again to say "thank you."

Earlier on the docks, sun-soaked,
coated in salt, you called me
a work of art,
so quick and quiet—
tripping over yourself.

The blue tinge of night drips onto us,
sitting close, talking shit
under our breath.
You thumb sand from my ankle.
No one notices.

Searching Fearless

Everyone here plants scrub roses.
Every good thing ends
with an opened screw top
or a cork. Streetlights turn on,
peach-tinting the aimless pink flowers—
thin like feathers, climbing post and rail fences,
and so many thorns. Bird-of-paradise colors
halo reflections in the darkened windows
on the darkened streets,
and I'm arms out, quick step spinning,
heel-toeing to the beach.
I scoop and toss sea-foam and sand
like fireworks dropping
to my sun-dried face. There are explosions
over the islands, explosions in my head—
sand between my teeth
tastes like spent gunpowder.

I'm older now than I've ever been,
cracking glasses into the sink,
broken chips stained in bitter puddles.
I fade barefoot to the wharf
in the early hours, shatter the star-fall
luminous harbor. I leave the rocks damp—
a slow climb back up—and melt into the granite
marking my heels like spilled pins.
My lips are only blue on the outside,
barnacle-stabbed hands only raw
on the outside.
I get whiskey cleaned,
pass out from the sting. I say thank you.

Opium Burns but Does Not Combust

The car burned,
wrapped in flames—
pops, whistles, breaking glass.
Smoke whispered into night sky,
the highway all ashes,
the breakdown lane all humid midsummer hell.

He stood wrapped in the smell of smoldering flowers,

smoke leaking from his busted lip then
back up through his swollen nose—
coughing black in the bed of his pickup.
Parked below the overpass
where we sat under the fire. Watching.

Sirens cut the two a.m. azure, and he asked
did I think—did the driver survive?

The smoke stays through midmorning.
The wrecked car hauled away,
dragging sparks on the pavement,
fender left behind.

I don't know who crashed, who lived.
I don't remember breathing.

After I Leave You at the Airport

I miss my exit
on the way out of Logan.
The tires are cold,
grooved pavement pinpricks
through my back and shoulders.

A blue-white-blue cruiser
blocks the right lane, five a.m. radios
harmonize in traffic:
Call in and win.

My hands are slow and chapped,
and none of us is caller twenty-five.
I get run through
by serpentine asphalt.

The lights in the Tunnel
burn fake and fluorescent.

Dementia Poem

My mother's father wrote Xs
and thought they were his name.
If we guessed right, his face
opened
like a palm, his hand steadied.
Once, I said *paperwork*—
he nodded,   shaking.

Something had erased from his body—
he knew that much.

First we asked questions,
then gave answers,
then named *nothing*,
and he
couldn't argue. We lied,   releasing him.

There were, there are
too many nothings.
Xs marking failures—
we didn't know how to know

what it meant when he used *nothing*
to describe nothing.

Highly Volatile Flammable Liquid

Things once in contact
are always in contact
but—

I wind up here somehow,
my hand just there,
missing it.

"Day one" is delicate—
an efficient illusion.
But right away, fewer glasses break.
Sour spots clear up.
A dustpan and disinfectant.

In a clean kitchen, there is one mistake,
and there is one certainty:

The first day is every day.
A space filled with nothing
is still a space
and still full.

Like I'm Well

If you feel sick,
focus on the horizon.
I knock myself down so easy.

Thatcher Light is dull this morning—
sleeping cement, salt-stained metal.
I know my directions, know
where the wind rushes from.
How it shifts. Can't you tell
I'm happy?
Are you sure?

I forget the start of days, I sink
and I settle.
The steps off the Light
were so smooth on the way down—
rocks algae-slick,
blurring the tide's spasms and eruptions.

I'll get back to the harbor
where the granite jetty holds off the storms.
It's just four more miles
in the hot sun.

Sewing

I ask, *Did you eat today?*

Toast, you say, but can't tell me
where the toaster is
or the butter. I sit with you because Papa
is not here,
because you forget
what hunger is.
But you don't forget the stitches.

You did this thing when you sewed:
folded the fabric, ran your thumb nail along the edge,
made a sharp crease—*that's your cutting line.*
You only ironed when it was finished.
Everything was edges and needles with you—

the creases and toothpicks for the baking, hair pins for the curlers,
never tweezers for splinters. My hands are scarred, too—
no blood but tomato. No bandage but flour and oil.
You asked, *Did you eat today?*

when I came home from school,
sat on the rug with the television low,
sun through the bay window.
My still-full Mickey Mouse lunch box
above my head. Back arched, looking up at you—
my anxious stomach giving me away.

Papa woke in his chair, got scali bread from the drawer,
spread two pieces with grape jelly
at the kitchen table.
I sat with him
and did not starve.

When I fit the scissors into the fold,
squeeze the blades to part the fibers,
you tell me, *keep going.* You choose thread,
open the machine's wooden lid—
the only way to make whole
is with needles, with food.
You cover me, still, keep me warm,
full, freshly ironed.

Watch the Birds for Warnings

Gulls weep on the roof,
then unravel over the harbor. There
is white fog—
these things are real.
I know because I don't dream much.
I am also real
          but tend to forget

and sleep with the windows wide open—
humid nights prickling my arms.
I could make a swift getaway.
I press my fingers into my lips, then
jerk them away
as if burned

by unaccountable fire. If the house ignited,
the birds would be first to flee
into cool Northeast air, never
look back at the riot of heat to see me

reaching my kissed hands through smoke.
          I did not keep the matches
          locked up
          or check the extinguisher for flaws—
I've never heeded caution.

I may want this: out of control
yellows, oranges, blues—
flames are reminders
that even gulls aren't permanent.
They will keep searching for safe places,
will never hush their wailing.

The Street Where We Lived Was Shaped Like a Horseshoe

Our neighbors used lighters to burn ants
on the sidewalk.
No magnifying glass bullshit—
faster to spark a flame,
faster
          to coil their bodies
          into black dust on the asphalt,
then crush them under frayed sneakers.
They slam into their houses
for ice pops in the freezer. And your brother,
that one time

chased rabbits with a shovel
          just to scare 'em,
just to see their white tails
book it under the shrubs
between our yards. I was scared of him,
but you know ...
                    I loved you a little back then.

You in front of your blue house—
I don't really remember your parents.

If I'd been paying better attention,
I would've taken you on long walks,
pushed you on the tire swing at the park
until you let go.
You know swings only slow
because the air pushes harder and harder
against them
in the opposite direction
          the higher they go.

And the notes don't sound sloppy—
it's just your calluses zipping the metal,
the friction of your hands
molding melody.

You were so skinny then, so tired.
Can you rest across the country?
One of these days, we'll both wake up
and know how it feels to breathe.

The Barn Rocks Are Covered with Broken Things

Rockweed steams iodine around the inlet,
empty lighthouse—a dark sentinel—
reflects sun and cove
down from its mirrored spine, tricking the eye.

White hot light beams down
on channel markers—
red right return keeping fishing boats off the sandbar
and the other unfortunate vessels buried

however many decades
or weeks ago.
Salt preserves their cores,
it's the outer layers that fray,

clutch weeds in the estuary.
Mussels clustered like sapphires grip tight,
shifting currents attack in variable weather
that sweeps through, leaving
just as quickly as it comes.

Midday and humid and brine
hangs in the air like horseflies
nibbling skin sprawled on the beach.
Like a singular animal, broad-shouldered birds
crown from the tidepool's edge, scattering in bulks
when kids rush up the rocks,
scattering shards of dead things
once dropped from great heights—

clam shells slap hot stones like gunpowder
popping white paper cases on pavement.

The gulls rise out of sync
splitting in different directions—
hollow barks riptiding their spines on the way out.

Addition

Look at the nail, not my hand—
the hammer goes
where your eye goes.
The nail, unmarred, shines silver
against the two-by-four.
My father shifts his weight,
his breath visible—*Go ahead, hit it.*
A ring, slight movement,
my elbows lock, full impact
in my hands—
I only hit it once.

My father shifts again,
there is his breath again,
says, *Go ahead* again
and again, the ring.
I will not strike
without his say so.
He says so three more times,
checks my work—
the nail is crooked.
With an adult-sized hammer,
he taps it ninety degrees up—
smiles, *Good,*
we'll work on making them straight.

If the Light Alarms You

It crawls over the blue edge—
the sun inching its way
          into new morning.
The Atlantic believes only in beginnings

and that edges
are only cliffs
if you don't see anything but the danger,
if you don't open your eyes
to see just how close the bottom is,

and, though the tracks curve hard right,
the car can't leave them. Chances are,
there will be soft grasses
at the end—hot and sweet—

or a splash of clean water.
You'll see. It's not too deep, but
if you get tired,
rest, your own air will keep you afloat—

you can be saved
by doing almost nothing at all.

In the Morning I Am Sober and Can See

Two swans circle off Bearskin Neck,
parting black ocean—
            lead glass before daylight wind stirs.
Their yellow feet looping a waltz,

necks folding angular
and stiff.
            I point my face
            beyond the breakwater.

Morning sun catches early frost on barnacles—
it's only October.
Their bodies already icicle sharp,
and they'll be here all winter—
stuck on the wharf ladders.

Lobster boats stay put,
their pot haulers clank a bittersweet clock—
            not a 1, 2, 3
            not a 2, 2, 3 either. There's no logic.
This bench, balanced on the uneven bulkhead,
needs a coat of paint.

From here, dawn could last forever.

Street Mary

Stuck between sidewalk cobblestones,
the scapular of Mary:
fogged, stained.
One hand at her heart,
the other at her pregnant belly,
sheathed in cross-hatched fabric—a river
of divinity
that she didn't expect. Mary,
you were baking when you realized,

slapping flat circles of barley dough
onto hot stones, child blooming in you,
smoke blooming from the oven. Mary,
you stood in the kitchen—
heat, grain, and sweat—knowing

questions of blood are
complicated. You knew
the answer to your own blood.

You were warned, Mary.
Still you mothered.

Mary, I memorized your prayer
in Sunday school, assumed you watched—
gaze gentle, hands quiet. I counted the beads,
crossed myself. Mary,
I am made of unblessed rivers—
rapid and winding.
Mary of the pierced heart, stuck through
seven times—blood and fire and
faded text. Mary,
I don't understand the rules,

but I keep you with me, Mary,
tucked in my pocket like my mother told me to.
Mary, hang on.

Mother

I never realize what I'm holding underneath
until you pull it all from me—
everything in all the hidden spaces—
and rinse the dirt away.
Show me from a distance
this new ring in my tree
spiraling back to you.

I am always wearing
some new someone, scattered
like marigold seeds you pry open
in the garden

where sun slicks your shoulders.
You save the largest blooms for me.

Turn My Will and Life Over

Time moves the same way
to get the lights up
as it does to set them down.
I've said *fight*
more than I've ever said *surrender.*
Beginning
just means there's more to do.

If the House Is Inclined to Collapse

Shingles peel from the roof—
just corners at first, then all at once
like sodden bandages. Nothing heals anything
          forever
          or completely.
These storms, they take their toll,

walls of gray blooming over breakwaters—
last light leaking over clouds, casting yellow on the cove
starting to swell.

A thick branch falls to half-frozen dirt—
new wood showing pale at the cracks—
and rolls to the water. These storms
wear it smooth, toss it back to a beach later, made special
for a mantle in a city
or some landlocked state far away from here.

Electric rain cupped in my hands absorbs
the first itch of lightning
that shakes the birds away,
their calls changing in time
to the whims of topography.
These storms are too violent
for bones of air—

the trick is to be ready,
retreat from what can't be predicted
          exactly
          or completely.
Put sandbags by the cellar door,
take umbrellas from the patio,

board up the windows facing the water—
things get lost here,
even when the wind dies, when the gulls come back.

They always leave traces
of their last meals—bones picked clean,
unhinged jaws salt-bleached
on fog-slicked planks. I leave them
where they lie, sharp and white.
I can count more colors in sopping Northeast gray
than any outsider can see when the clouds pass,
when everything settles, surprised by its own survival.

Handwriting

I had the most trouble with *d's*—
swooping the letter in one stroke,
loop first, then straight line up
like checking a box.
The unruly flourish always slanted outside the lines.
Then, Dad's eraser,
wiping out the answers.

I know they're right—
doesn't matter if I can't read them.

He felt the pressure points—
I still hold my pencil too tight—
ran his finger over sentences, eyes following,
checking.
I got mixed up between print and cursive—

should the letters separate?
Curl? Twine around each other
in knots? Too many knots to make them
all the same. Connecting them
made the work faster,
but shortcuts were not allowed.

My father writes notes in block letters,
labels diagrams—plans
for rebuilding, altering,
refinishing—
he takes months
to flush the edges, keep the brush strokes straight.

No shortcuts.
It wasn't about how quickly
I could fill the green paper
with its oversized blue lines.
It was never about the answers.

It was about the cabinet doors closing smooth,
Dad saying, *Hear that? Nothing.*
It was about the words—rewritten three times if I had to—
coming out clean and about the
the floors he built beneath me being level.

Testament

I want to die by the Atlantic Ocean—
end my good long life
down on the beach, sun
warming my face until sand floods my eyes
and catches in my throat.
I'll smile

at the autumns when I
counted tapping sleet on vinyl siding, November
leaking through window sashes.
There were many
terrible haircuts, failures
to roller-skate—my hands
burned raw in the driveway.
And there was my dog, sleeping
heavy on the rug in front of the oven.

I want to die where the sun rises—
where sky opens
with pale blue—instead of sets
in riots of West Coast orange. Where mornings
are cold most of the year,

and spring ice on the beach
takes a long, long time to melt. I want
the metal tang of low tide
clinging to me
like the taste of lemon candy
singeing my tongue—I'm not sure
if I ever liked it. Maybe
it was only the color—

the hesitant yellow tiptoeing
the shallows like seabirds that
find me buried and pull me
out from my body to sea.

A Decade Difference

I call your name, and you don't answer.
I call your name your name your name,
                    and the more I say it, the more it means
                    across the silence
of the crown of your head, poised on your flower-petal neck.

You keep blooming,
unfolding yourself. I love you for that.

For not asking if I want to come.
All of this?
It's yours now,

as if I had anything to do with the words
flying out from your peach mouth

making the world.

I close my eyes against you,
and there is the red, the yellow burning,
the blueprint of what was illuminated—
                    lines and figures and the way you stand:
                    weight all on one side,
the day curved to your hip,
light skipping across your angles.

If we never met, would you know me anyway?
What if, when you were born, I was even older?

Anamnesis

My grandmother pulls my hair
tight back, brushing as she goes.
There is so much of it,
and so tangled,
and *where did this blond come from.*
We are cooking today—
it needs to be *out of my face.*

Acid scent of tomato slices out from the can.
Nana pours whole romas into the mill. *Turn those*
over her shoulder—
she lets me sit on the counter,
linoleum edge digging the back of my knees.
I grind seeds away from the meat.
She is head and shoulders in the cabinet
below me—metal pop of pans shifting—

looking for the *big pot.* My fingers are stained pink
from dipping—I like tomatoes best
when they taste like the vine smells:
sort of hollow and the sun.
There was a tablespoon of sugar
in every gravy Nana made.

Electric stove coils red,
I scrub my hands
back to February vacation white.
Let it sit for the day, leave it,
but Papa lifts the lid anyway,
and we sweep a wooden spoon
through the simmering red
every time we pass through the kitchen.

The wallpaper was brown and tan—
women filling baskets with wheat,
their hair braided tight under straw hats.

Charlie

When you died, I was not there
in piles of your *Reader's Digest* Westerns,
fruit preserves, junk mail. It happened
just after Christmas. We'd bought you socks,
but you didn't *need any more things,*
wouldn't wish ninety-two on anyone.

When you died, I thought you
might wake up, say, *Just kidding!*
Getting older doesn't kill you,
you just get better at fooling people.
You planned your own funeral—
didn't want the fuss. My father

dressed you in flannel—
reading glasses around your neck,
pine cones and branches and Tennessee irises.
You took me fishing in Ardmore—drifting

the muddy Mississippi current.
Watch out for snakes—they'll jump right in the boat,
you said, then two-note chuckled
at my wide eyes.
I always liked your aluminum canoe.
You always liked your garden
more than you liked most people—

solitary king rooted firmly in East Boston.
You gave heirloom tomatoes,
peaches, and green beans
like talismans.

Once, we picked grapes in your backyard—
spiders building nets between the
vines and leaves, popping out
when I reached for the red and purple fruit
we collected in plastic buckets.

The thing about wine grapes
is, they're tough. You don't really chew them,
just crush out all the sweetness
before discarding the skin.

At Pop's funeral, his buddy tells me the deer head is mine if I want it.

A full rack blossoms
from late spring scrub—
not even the crows touch the heap of brown
on the hillside, sheathed in misted fur
and flies.
It just fell like that, the old buck, and

the farmer left it—*the field will do its work,*
bring the body back to dirt.
Warmer days speed decay.
No fancy mount for this one, just lingering frost
on the slow-thawing earth, clamoring
into the next season like Pop's van
clamoring fast up our street
back from Maine—buck's rack rattling aluminum.
He stood all silver beard and hair tucked
under a cap, full height sloped to one side
on the front steps asking Dad: *You want any of this?*

A month in his cabin—
he needs a shower, his armchair.
He napped once on the highway
after a slow day through snow—
the white powder falling thick like his stories.
Pop is only as old as I am able to see him,

old as backyard running barefoot,
leaves sticking everywhere,
my mother shaking out our sweatshirts
before breakfast—two eggs and cornbread
and *stop adding sugar to the mix.*

He cleans the deer, mounts the head in the kitchen
up north
where snow blocks the door.

But everything melts eventually.
That deer in the field took eight weeks
to rot back to earth.

Gold

It was always cold outside. A warm tray
covered with foil, salt
turning ice to puddles—avoid them,
we are wearing our
good shoes.
The shades are up at Christmas—

Santa and Mrs. Claus wave
slow in the bay window.
Red dress, apron—her spectacles slip,
he's in his rocking chair,
list on his lap, quill, missing—
kicked away in the garage, I'm sure.

Blast of hot air and garlic—
yelling from the stove, Nana
says, *Put the food on the pool table, don't*
slam the dishes down.
Where's my baby? pulls me to her chest.
Get a tablespoon. Add the sugar to the gravy.
The ziti will be overcooked. Again.

Papa is downstairs.
He pulls out sambuca, pours
two fingers, drops in ice,
touches the tumbler to his lips.
Take a whiff, he says.
Lick the edge of the glass. My eyes
make him laugh, squinting.
We have been stealing
pizzellis *for the party* all week.

How can I explain grandparents
or holidays
without turkey?
They taught me
to speak their Italian—
I know all the curse words.

Food, there is too much food. There is
just enough food. Papa shares
salt peanuts with me. I drink wine
and ginger ale from a Solo cup—I don't know
if I like it, but I'm twelve and
am allowed. The kids run circles,

only eat the frosting
from the cookies. Three choruses of
"Domenick the Donkey" before Papa—
also Domenic—says they're *giving him agida,*
knock it off, bites his flat hand,
waves them away—they shriek and smile.
My sister in my lap
gums Topo Gigio's nose,

Papa sings the wrong lyrics to Dean Martin,
Nana *hasn't sat down yet*.
I am not ready to talk about
when they stopped
dancing in the kitchen.
One Christmas Eve, Nana teaches me
to trick shot the cue ball—
it goes one way, the eight, another.
I beat my cousin—first time.

He hammers my knuckles
with the yellow number one.
Papa sits him outside
until he shivers—blue lips, damp sneakers.
He doesn't speak to me
for the rest of the night
or forever.

I walk by their house now,
am bundled against December, against
the feeling of away.
I step in slush
before I see it,
keep the shades up all year,
use sugar to cut the acid.

The Heart Works the Same in Most Bodies

The Helena hummingbird
is the smallest in the world.
They're only called hummingbirds because
their hearts beat so fast and don't give out,

and they can't curb their consumption,
slurping sugar from gardens pocking suburbs,
sucking from perfect dendrobium
choking the weeds and wild.
The small white flowers are well-groomed, methodical—

they tangle and constrict—
they don't stitch the fractures whole,
they do the tearing.

In summer, neighborhood kids dig fingers
into soil to get to the other side
the other side other side,

giggling while they work—patterned, like clocks.
Half-moon dirt under their nails,
they knead the doughy mulch,
and soft spots give way to bigger holes.

A valve opens
then closes, like it's important.
But once a man lived without a heart for 555 days,
and he turned out okay
in the end.

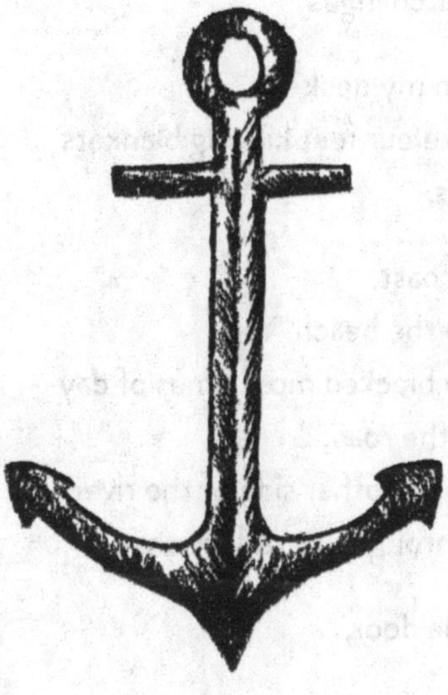

I imagine more conversations with you than I have with you—

and it's worse when I'm driving,
when you're not walking
past all the same trees
splitting sidewalks on Lowell Street.

Do you ever really leave the place you come from?
How's the city?
The gridlock never changes

and your cheek on my neck
never stays put like our feet kicking blankets
down to our knees.

Here, I am open coast,
and you don't like the beach. You,
with your city sky blocked most times of day—
metal rails above the road,
bridge lighting up the other side of the river.
Once, it passed through our reflections—

you, framed in one door,
me in the other,
separating to black,
then together in worn out incandescence.
Ghosts in the grime.
How's your day?

You might say
it's fine.
You might ride the subway
alone. Might listen to that song we sing in the car

when you visit (or come home,
depending on how you look at it).
Is it cold there?
It’s starting to feel like fall here.

Old Salt

It's March everywhere,
but it cuts different
in the East,

cuts my coat wide open—I miss so much
keeping my arms to myself.

Lingering brown snowbanks line the streets
running parallel through town—
they hide cans crushed flat,
cover broken glass.
And next month,

just sand
where the ice used to be—that gravelly junk
the city spreads
on the one good beach
where it's too toxic to swim.

The gulls mourn
like they know what I keep giving up.
Like they've given up, too.

I zip my jacket—it's cold,
night's coming on quick.

Late May

If it were easy—
like a step up from the ground to the porch—
then I wouldn't be standing here
on the quiet pavement rocking heel toe,
pretending. I'd be kicked up,
swinging bench and lemonade, curiosity soothed
by heat off the front lawn.

But tonight, it's raining,
nothing is still—shivering, wind-driven wet.
My finger traces lines through air like mountains against horizon—
some peaks take the shapes of pulses
too fast to ignore. Chains on the swing heart-beat back and forth,
swaying easy—lulling the trees still
in the streetlight glow.

After Dinner

I watched the traffic on the way home—
my breath restless dogwood blooming
across cold glass—pale petals
straining for light.
I am used to this.

Used to you collecting me,
then moving me
back and forth over long distances. Used to you

folding your words and legs beneath you,
your sinking shoulders,
and the keys you swallow.

You left your coat on a kitchen chair—
I hadn't left room on the hooks—
and you put your shoes in the closet
before washing your face.

Tell me the truth:
was that your soft breath
against my back? Or just the breeze
through the open window
finding its way closer to me?

In This Small Town, the Road We Drive

We quick drive the loop, disturb the dark
country-club peace—our families,
our friends' families
can't afford it.
We don't roll down the windows
this time of year. Late winter raw—
it's cold, and the fog—

I don't try to see past it.
I turn the headlights
all the way off.
White mist curtain slips
over the hood, your shaking tenor
slips over the stereo—
I don't try to hear past you.
Past stories run parallel
like harmonics—not quite the note
but a shortcut to getting there.

You come and leave so often
I can't keep track,
often don't know
we are in the same state.
I keep off the highway—moving faster
makes us messy, and you talk less.
You don't sing.

Wailing through old speakers
on these Peabody back roads,
no curfew now, but whose clock
mattered even then? And anyway,
it's never really quiet here,
between two interstates,
population bursting town lines,

a brook bursting the drains—
the square floods
every time it rains.
Pretend we don't notice
one thirty a.m. in this parking lot
surrounded by the muddy fields,
the bare apple trees of Brooksby Farm—
from here, the mall light horizon glow
looks like sunrise.

Only the Year-rounders See the Harbor Almost Empty

Traffic shakes on the rain-pocked windshield—
headlights lens flare
on the bridge—
no passenger, and it's too cold

for this time of year,
or what it should be—spring:
it's some bullshit.

Through whipping slats of
wrought-iron railing—broken reel
on a boat in the harbor.
Funny,
how close to real ocean it is
without catching
any of the wind. No one else

is back north yet.
Even the lone cutter—barely hugged
by the jetty—is empty
for a few more months.
Metallic scent of low tide
floats around crossbeams and up,

and I take the long way—
road empty, road open,
my mouth drinking
seaweed threads from the breeze. I think
about driving to your house.

Lyme Disease in Essex County

The blood started at the eighth fairway.
The cops just followed it over the snow
through mangled branches—a record-setting storm—
and into our neighbor's backyard

where Dad and I cut through up to the golf course,
collecting slices no one bothered to look for.
Breaking the trees, I'd run to scatter
patches of Canada geese crowding the water hazards
still slushed over in late winter.

Fog puffed from melting snow,
crisp and rough under my boots—they weren't quite waterproof—
my feet shoved into thick socks shoved into sandwich bags.
None of us—the kids on my street—
were allowed to walk the municipal woods alone
until high school
when no one watched which shortcuts we took.

The trails are still overgrown,
lined with snuffed fires, sleeping bags, empty fifths—
our parents were probably right,
we shouldn't have been there

where our neighbor most likely hunted even before
dropping that doe on a folding table
in his open garage
and playing ignorant to the PPD.

I'm not sure what happened after that—
the deer population had gotten out of hand,
other cities extended hunting season.

But he used a bow
in an unlisted town
on private property in February,
and well—

Danvers State Before the Year Ends

I drive up Christmas Eve morning, past scrub
pressed through melted snow—
all the fields shine, reflecting. I forgot my sunglasses—

I drive up because I'm meeting my family for breakfast
at Nick and Andy's,
and they're running late, so I have time
to drink another coffee.

I keep talking about this as if I know anything,
as if I've been there, like there's something I learned besides
my great grandfather died there,
and the one time she visited, my mother
was scared
by how he was living,
or how he really wasn't.
Her aunts couldn't get him to eat—

I drive up because,
even though they knocked it all down for luxury apartments
but they kept the main façade, bigger than I've seen in pictures—
it pulses like it knows
the people living here
don't know

what happened here
when everything went to shit, which it really did—

but I drive
up through a farm, behind the Lahey annex on Route 62,
past a boulder with aluminum letters reading *Halstead Danvers*
because I can't stop
thinking about what we all think

of this place, why we all think it,
or think we know it and are afraid,

which is why I drive up,
but I don't visit the graves.

Gesticular Fixation

Someone kept setting fire to the playgrounds—

burnt holes through neon polyethylene slides,
sharp melted strands hanging through
like ice off gutters.

When the sun hit, the singed bits
smelled like high school anarchists,
like hormones, ninety-nine cent Richdale lighters
and adolescent sweat

worked up running from Peabody cops
into the woods edging the reservoir by Route 1.

There's always one free couch left out on Pulaski Street
in somewhere suburbia—
where I grew up,
folks in my development were afraid of one thing or another
    permeating from outside.

        Really, it was just kids TP'ing houses on Halloween
        or prom night, draping silly string over wooden fences

in the fall. Leaves blocked drains, and the pipes were too small—
yellow and brown stuck in grates bolted over either end
to keep other shit out.

        I never did understand it—

the brook trickled most of the year
until one good storm
sent it over the streets.
        And the tide coming in,
                it hurts.

Salem Harbor feeds the canal
into North River then flows under the town center
to Proctor's Brook.
Storm surge, torrential rain—trapped
in our neighborhood for three days,

we watched the news to see friends floating down Foster
Street
in tubes, and we laughed about it—
half of them were still sick when school reopened.
The rain stopped eventually—

orange vests cut trees, dredged soil, took out branches,
shook our windows with diamond saws
to cut the upended pavement. It covers three directions
of my coiled-chain city.
Once the mall closed, we had nowhere to go,
so we went nowhere over and over
the asphalt over the tide, tender as a fresh bruise.

Some kids
used their brothers' or sisters' IDs at Paddy Kelly's
for High Lifes and wine coolers.
The rest of us drove the circle,
        screaming our throats out the windows
        of beater Toyotas,

        voices skimming the tide
        rushing into the pipes
        crisscrossed through the city's weak foundation.

A senior in drama club drove a Jeep Wrangler.
                                I loved that car.
My first time was in a Chevy Blazer
in the school parking lot,

                but I still get pissed if someone calls me a
                townie.

He lit a candle in the cupholder,
kept his hoodie on, and the cops
left us alone. It was raining then, too,
early June, maybe a Tuesday night.

He was flunking out, I lied to him
about getting straight A's. Everything was all sweet,
    but sugar ignites if heated fast enough, hot enough.
    That December, someone left a burner on,
    flames shot from the back room of the candy store
    over trees three blocks from my bedroom window.
            When it burned, the smoke
            smelled like chocolate and latex paint.
    Industrial ash drifted into the brook, left it grayer.

This one kid, the year after I graduated—
I think he was a junior?—brought in a BB gun
and shot it at some kids between second and third period.
I heard he got a couple days suspension.

His intention was pretty clear:
shoot your way out.

Sometimes in winter the hills up to school were so slick
we got let out at the bottom on Lowell Street
and had to walk.
Traffic backed up for miles—all the miles to the Square
hovering over the tide.

Wouldn't it be funny
if someday it sank?

My hometown—it's like a stab in the hand
with a number two pencil:
the lead sticks around years and years
after the puncture heals.

Shannon Beach

I couldn't see my feet or arms
through sand he kicked up
from the bottom I couldn't reach.
He had two life rings,
and I just treaded.
The water wasn't any cooler
than the air.

He reached for me, said *hold on,*
but he didn't hold back.
When I came up
spitting silt through my teeth,
out my nose,
we both laughed and laughed

'til the sound floated away from us.
I swam to stand up,
he said I was too far, called
come back, hooked his arms
through mine, told me
keep kicking,
you can't be tired yet.

The First Humid Day of Summer

Even a good day isn't
a good day.
His friend killed himself.
Mine did, too,

but I don't say it—doesn't matter,
just someone's kid is dead. And someone
is trimming the bushes outside in the rain,
cursing when the trimmer jams in the wet.

He's been awake for hours,
not from the noise in the yard—
it was the cat
scratching the bedroom door.

She sits on the windowsill
swatting a plant.
He's cleaning out his closet,
throwing old clothes into the trash.

September Has Lasted a Year

I can't run and stand straight
at the same time—the pressure of
too much space behind me.

I am almost through tall grass,
toes stepped to the water
ready to swim—

almost. Cool September nights
make it all so cold that
I feel it in my knees,
aching, always,
from something I can't quite name.

I sink up to my ankles on the beach—
the muddy shallows full of holes.
A spotted dog bounces through tide pools,
yapping at an eider—
he almost catches it.

There's a Waterfall in Brooklyn

Gray morning bleeds
through autumn drying out
from the steady mist that went all night,
multiplying headlights through Connecticut
by thousands, their glow
snaking through stone tunnels
before hitting the Hudson.

Outside, trees and dogs and sirens
talk to each other—it's a nice day now
in the park, a plane cuts the clouds,
and mid-October leaves decide whether it's time.
Paper sounds of animals in scrub rustle
through air traffic hum,
lift sweet leaf rot from the soil and stream.
Chain-links fence the water below—

it's a short drop down, a drop
that wouldn't hurt much.
For once, this is the same place—
our feet still and solid on crooked stone steps,
we look over field after field
bordered by brick and mortar.
They say motion sickness goes away
once the motion stops.

Abyssal Overturning

Forty degrees in the city,
no ice on the river yet,
and me: bare wrists and windburned cheeks
waiting for a cab

on the parkway.
          Something hovers off the bulkhead.
          I shrink it from a distance
          between two fingers—
          marble just past my nose,
          eyes crossed to keep it in focus.
          Water sifts through its fanning jaws—
          open like holes in the lining of your jacket.

I could have sewn them shut—
just some sturdy thread,
just a simple whipstitch.

All the Tracks Ripped Up but One

Trains run through the Square
maybe once every other month,
traveling too slow.

Two whistle blasts—I've never cared
what the cars carry, just that they back up traffic
for half an hour. One year—it was early—a freighter
knocked a dumpster into a closed-down pizza joint.
Someone said Waste Management misplaced it,

and someone else said it was the tracks,
heaved up by frost. The bar owner next door
just shrugged. *Doesn't matter—*

fall floods are worse than trains
shoving trash through the walls.

In this town, they wait
until the next thing breaks and don't worry
about what never gets fixed.
Let the plows keep tearing up the pavement
and the schools shed their bricks season by season.

The other rails were labeled *beyond repair*.
Where they used to be,
the asphalt is darker than the rest of the roads—
concentric loops across the center of town
under squealing, unpredictable wheels.

None of them has hit anything since,
and mostly everyone forgot it happened.

Barnacle

Black coffee and the wind picks up.
Boats in the harbor—their moorings loosed
from bottom sand—pitch a stuttered rise,
a stuttered fall. Frantic salt water

saturates the air, a dingy batters the rocks,
batters to splinters.

Wind shakes the house,
a storm comes through, and the screen door—
yanked crooked last year—
thrashes the vinyl siding on broken hinges.

Coffee spills on the counter—
no dishrags in the drawer—
and spools around a pot of marram grass
moving in drafts
through the old walls.

Terns dive toward the rocks,
rolling like kids' marbles out to sea.

Power still burns though the kitchen bulbs,
but there are candles in the windows
because I know—
because the neighbor's trees are swaying.

Commuting in Late January

Four hawks perch miles apart
                    by the highway
kneading their feet in fresh kills,
but state troopers
only watch the speed guns,

and drivers
only watch for state troopers
on the backsides of overpasses.

The woman
in the Volvo next to me
in traffic
at medium speed
pets her dog sitting up in the passenger seat—

the car is full of clear bags
full of clothes.
                    Hers? And where
                    will it all go now?

It's the long haulers
that slow us over the hills—the weight of the trailers,
the uncomfortable early evening
glare—we are forced
to feather our brakes.
I'm squinting
                    at the highway horizon, blurred
                    license plates . . .
                    infinite loops off the pavement.

High Functioning

There's a point on 127 where the road
banks down and to the left, past a beach
that disappears at high tide. At dusk,
with no perception of depth,
you could almost be driving straight into wet horizon—
I ride my brakes on the hill.
Last year
I saw this section of road
most often at two a.m.
The moon slithered
in bright strips
across the indigo harbor. So gently,
like it couldn't
just drown me if it wanted.
Last year I sped up around this curve,
then coasted through the tighter turns that come next.
It felt—I kept waking up carrying misplaced days
with pins-and-needle hands, my head
dead-weighted with black hours and my mouth
stained bitter.
It is impossible to count all the dust that floats along the ceiling.
It is impossible to stay alive
while you're dying.

Building was easy—

it's the breaking that takes practice.
Walls don't come down without making a mess.
Debris always follows
when something crumbles—

always roots grown through rock, always
the unexpected tangle
of something alive.
The way to start
is not at the top, sledge hammer in hand.
Begin at the bottom, lift.
It's near impossible—

the point is,
there's a way.

Quick-rinse the dust under the hose,
leave the heavier pieces—
they'll disappear into the landscape,
make new hills.
You see? See how they roll and catch the sun?

Acknowledgments

Like me, these poems had a lot of growing up to do from their shitty first drafts. I've spent the last five years (or was it a decade?) crafting and unmaking and gluing them back together again, and I'm grateful for all the time I've had with them, taking up space in my brain and on my desk.

First and foremost, I have to offer endless thanks to the folks at Salem Writers Group for reading and commenting on the first drafts and the second drafts... and the fifth drafts. J.D. Scrimgeour, who has been a guiding hand for over twenty years, thank you for every single big and little thing that you've contributed to my life in poetry. How lucky I was to walk into your class on my first day at Salem State, drenched from the rain, and get to tell stories for years and years after. And to Jennifer Martelli, who was a kindred spirit in so many ways but most especially in the Italian-ness of it all: huge hugs and huger thank-yous. You are so loved, and you are so very missed.

These poems exist together because of the incredible group of people with whom I had the privilege of writing at UNH. Even though our time was cut short in the spring of 2020, you all remain the most influential band of writers I've worked with. Thank you to the English faculty for your guidance and support: Tom Payne, who taught me to wonder what makes this Tuesday different from any other Tuesday; David Blaire, whose unwavering curiosity about the words on the page propelled me into examining poems in a way I never had before; and my twin pillars, David Rivard and Mekeel McBride, for the road map to bringing my world to the page and my work to life. Without all of you, I'm certain that I would still be a poet, but I'm also pretty certain I wouldn't be a very good one. Theresa Monteiro, my soul sister in poetry, who is a powerhouse in so many ways–you are so special to me, I can't fully explain it. And Danley Ramirez, the kindest soul with a talent for the weird and wonderful.

Though they're not with me anymore, at least in this physical space, I continue to thank my grandparents–Nana, Papa, and Pop–for remaining unwavering figures throughout my life and now in my memories. Whether food, off-key singing, or long-winded stories, I stand a little taller–a little stronger–whenever I think of you. My parents, Ella and Len, who when confronted with a creative spirit (that spends way too much time in her own head) watered and nurtured it like some sort of complex houseplant: thank you a million billion gazillion times. To my little sister, Becky Jo, the fire to my water, my complete opposite and my perfect match: I love you so very much. And to Frank because, well, you get me.

There are so many other poets and humans I have encountered and that I experience life with every day, and I hope you know how valued you are and how thankful I am for having brushed arms or brushed years with you.

This book is full of brokenness and joy, and I would like to shed love on those, including myself, who caused both. I hope these poems honor the mistakes we all made and the hurts we all caused. They make us–they've made me–wholly human.

Finally, to you, who have read this far, thank you for taking your time with these words. I hope you've underlined some phrases you liked, scribbled your own thoughts in the margins, or drawn a stick figure or shooting star inside the cover. Thank you for being a part of this book's life.

Title Index

T

W

First Line Index

www.ingramcontent.com/pod-product-compliance
Lightning Source LLC
LaVergne TN
LVHW030922080826
845145LV00013B/3020

* 9 7 8 1 5 9 4 9 8 2 2 2 4 *